Commitment, Compassion, Consecration:
Inspirational Quotes of Theodore M. Hesburgh, C.S.C.

Selected and Compiled by
Thomas J. Mueller and Charlotte A. Ames

Our Sunday Visitor Publishing Division
Our Sunday Visitor, Inc.
Huntington, Indiana 46750

ISBN: 0-87973-430-2
LCCCN: 88-63542

PRINTED IN THE UNITED STATES OF AMERICA

Cover design by Rebecca J. O'Brien

430

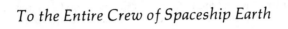

To the Entire Crew of Spaceship Earth

Acknowledgments

The compilers wish to express their deepest gratitude to Reverend Theodore M. Hesburgh, C.S.C., who has, by his life's work, made this little volume possible. We also gratefully acknowledge the generous contributions of many librarians and archivists throughout the United States and other countries who have contributed copies of Father Hesburgh's addresses.

We wish to render words of special thanks to William Kevin Cawley, Peter J. Lysy and Charles R. Lamb, Archivists, University of Notre Dame; Ruth Quinn, College of Engineering; G. Margaret Porter, Linda Gregory and Mollie H. Toole, Theodore M. Hesburgh Library; Richard W. Conklin, Assistant Vice President, University Relations; and M. Bruce Harlan, Director of Photography, University Relations.

We also deeply appreciate the kind support of many other individuals who have contributed so much in so many ways to assist us in bringing this work to light.

The author and publisher are grateful to the following for excerpts from their materials used in this work: • University of Notre Dame, for *Patterns for Educational Growth: Six Discourses at the University of Notre Dame*, by Theodore M. Hesburgh, C.S.C. Notre Dame, Ind.: University of Notre Dame Press, © 1958; reprinted by permission of University of Notre Dame. • Yale University, for *The Humane Imperative: A Challenge for the Year 2000*, by Theodore M. Hesburgh, C.S.C. New Haven: Yale University Press, © 1974; reprinted by permission of Yale University. • Andrews and McMeel, for *The Hesburgh Papers: Higher Values in Higher Education*, by Theodore M. Hesburgh, C.S.C. Kansas City: Andrews and McMeel, © 1979; reprinted by permission of Andrews and McMeel. • University of Notre Dame, for *More Thoughts for Our Times* (1964), *Thoughts IV* (1967), *Vision and Faith: The Inner Life of Notre Dame* (1985), by Theodore M. Hesburgh, C.S.C., published by the Department of Public Relations and Information, University of Notre Dame Press, © 1985; reprinted by permission of Notre Dame University.

Other sources include: • American Council on Education, for *Contemporary Issues in Higher Education*, edited by John B. Bennett and J. W. Peltason, 247-66, "The Role of the Academy in a Nuclear Age," by Theodore M. Hesburgh, C.S.C. New York: Macmillan Publishing Company, Inc., © 1985. • Random House, for *What Works For Me: 16 CEOs Talk About Their Careers and Commitments*, by Thomas R. Horton, 151-77, "Theodore M. Hesburgh, C.S.C." New York: Random House Business Division, © 1986.

Table of Contents

FOREWORD

Father Theodore M. Hesburgh, C.S.C., retired as president of the University of Notre Dame after serving in that position for thirty-five years. During that period, which represents the longest tenure of any president of an American institution of higher education, he made significant contributions to the educational endeavors of the nation. His voice was especially forceful in the area of Catholic higher education during three and one-half decades of change in the Church and in society.

Father Hesburgh's public service career was most distinguished, and involved him in virtually every social issue of his time, including civil rights, the peaceful use of atomic energy, amnesty for Vietnam offenders, immigration reform, the pursuit of peace, and many others.

Service to four popes and fourteen presidential commissions provided Father Hesburgh with unusual opportunities to study and address these issues from his special perspective as a deeply committed Christian, a challenging educator and a tireless advocate for the needy.

This book contains representative thoughts on many of these issues and concerns which came to Father Hesburgh's attention, and to which he devoted a life of extraordinary service.

To fellow educators he is an insightful colleague; to men and women interested in issues of justice and peace he is a tireless promoter of dialogue and an example of commitment; and to those who are concerned with improving the lot of the poor he is a willing coworker. Above all, Father Hesburgh is a Holy Cross priest who serves his God and Church with great joy, competence and distinction.

This book contains an insightful collection of Father Hesburgh's thoughts for every reader. For those who know him well, it will serve as a source of meditation and inspiration as well.

Edward A. Malloy, C.S.C.
President
University of Notre Dame

PREFACE

The purpose of this compilation of quotations from the works of Theodore M. Hesburgh is to present but a few of the timeless thoughts and ideas of this remarkable priest. In reading his books, commencements and other major addresses, and from listening to him speak to the faculty and students at Notre Dame for more than twenty years, it is apparent that Hesburgh's major goal in life was simply to be a good priest. A good priest administers to the spiritual, mental, and physical well-being of people in any possible way.

Because of his intellectual ability, his facility with languages, organizational skills, his vision, and enormous energy, he was able to accomplish more than all of his predecessors. The most amazing part of this story is that in addition to transforming a rather small university known principally for its athletic prowess to a major research university of outstanding academic quality, he also made major contributions to the nation, the Catholic Church, and the Third World through his unprecedented public service career. The biographical sketch presented in the introduction highlights many of his accomplishments at Notre Dame and elsewhere. As most of us do, Hesburgh responded to the forces exerted upon him by the world and society in which he lived. Thus he made important contributions to the areas of human rights, the peaceful uses of atomic energy, and higher education. A chronology of events which probably influenced Hesburgh to respond to the needs of others is shown in the introduction. This chronology begins with his birth, May 25, 1917, and ends with his retirement as president of the University of Notre Dame in 1987. Hesburgh's current work focuses on the International Peace Institute which he founded in 1985.

The life and work of Hesburgh has been and will continue to be an inspiration to all people: young and old, rich and poor, majority and minority, educated and un-educated. It is very clear that above all else, this man, this priest exemplified the values of commitment, compassion, and consecration.

Father Hesburgh on the porch of Sorin Hall, 1967

The idea for this book was born of the reflective atmosphere which surrounded Father Hesburgh's retirement as president of the University of Notre Dame in the spring of 1987. It is an attempt to provide a wide audience with a glimpse of Hesburgh the priest through his thoughts, both written and spoken. It is clear that throughout his life it was his deep faith in God and his desire to do the work of God that provided both the drive and continuity needed to accomplish so much. The biographical sketch and chronology of events which follow provide some of the background needed to begin to put Hesburgh's life in perspective.

Biographical Perspective

Father Hesburgh was born in Syracuse, New York, on May 25, 1917, the son of Anne Murphy Hesburgh and Theodore Bernard Hesburgh, an executive of the Pittsburgh Plate Glass Company. A brother, James, graduated from Notre Dame in 1955, received his M.B.A. from Harvard in 1960 and is now president of James L. Hesburgh International, Inc., in Los Angeles, California. Notre Dame's president emeritus has two sisters, Mrs. Robert O'Neill, Cazenovia, New York, and Mrs. John Jackson, Syracuse, New York. A third sister, Mrs. Alton Lyons of Oneida, New York, died in 1957.

Father Hesburgh was educated at Notre Dame and the Gregorian University in Rome, from which he received a bachelor of philosophy degree in 1939. He was ordained a priest of the Congregation of Holy Cross in Sacred Heart Church on the Notre Dame campus June 24, 1943, by Bishop John F. Noll of Fort Wayne. Following his ordination, Father Hesburgh continued his study of sacred theology at The Catholic University of America, Washington, D.C., receiving his doctorate (S.T.D.) in

1945. He joined the Notre Dame faculty the same year, and served as chaplain to World War II veterans on campus in addition to his teaching duties in the Religion Department. He was appointed the head of the department in 1948, and the following year was appointed executive vice-president to Reverend John J. Cavanaugh, C.S.C., University president. At the age of 35 in June 1952, he was named the 15th president of Notre Dame.

Highlighting a lengthy list of awards to Father Hesburgh is the Medal of Freedom, the nation's highest civilian honor, bestowed on him by President Lyndon Johnson in 1964. He has received numerous awards from education groups, among them the prestigious Meiklejohn Award of the American Association of University Professors in 1970. This award, which honors those who uphold academic freedom, recognized Father Hesburgh's crucial role in blunting the attempt of the Nixon Administration in 1969 to use federal troops to quell campus disturbances.

On more than one occasion, Father Hesburgh found himself the first Catholic priest to serve in a given position. Such was the case during the years he was a director of the Chase Manhattan Bank and a trustee (later, chairman) of the Rockefeller Foundation. Also, his appointment as ambassador to the 1979 United Nations Conference on Science and Technology for Development was the first time a priest had served in a formal diplomatic role for the United States government.

The author of several monographs, Notre Dame's president emeritus has written two books during the past decade and a half, *The Humane Imperative: A Challenge for the Year 2000*, published in 1974 by the Yale University Press, and *The Hesburgh Papers: Higher Values in Higher Education*, published in 1979 by Andrews,

McMeel, Inc. A consistent theme in these and other writings is a vision of the contemporary Catholic university as touching the moral as well as the intellectual dimensions of scholarly inquiry. "The Catholic University should be a place," he wrote, "where all the great questions are asked, where an exciting conversation is continually in progress, where the mind constantly grows as the values and powers of intelligence and wisdom are cherished and exercised in full freedom."

Hesburgh was a national leader in the field of education, serving on many commissions and study groups examining matters ranging from public funding of independent colleges and universities to the role of foreign languages and international studies in higher education. As president of the International Federation of Catholic Universities from 1963 to 1970, he led a movement to redefine the nature and mission of the contemporary Catholic university. His stature as an elder statesman in American higher education is reflected in his 112 honorary degrees, the most ever awarded to one person.

Notre Dame's president emeritus has served four Popes, three as permanent Vatican City representative to the International Atomic Energy Agency in Vienna from 1956 to 1970. At the request of Pope Paul VI, he built in 1972 an Ecumenical Institute at Tantur, Jerusalem, which Notre Dame continues to operate. Paul VI also appointed him head of the Vatican representatives attending the 20th anniversary of the U.N.'s Human Rights Declaration in Teheran, Iran, in 1968, and six years later a member of the Holy See's United Nations delegation. In 1983, Father Hesburgh was appointed by Pope John Paul II to the Pontifical Council for Culture, charged with finding ways in which the saving message of the Gospel can be preached effectively in the world's variegated cultures.

The public service career of Notre Dame's president emeritus was as distinguished as his educational contributions. Father Hesburgh held 14 presidential appointments over the years, and they involved him in virtually all the major social issues — civil rights, peaceful uses of atomic energy, campus unrest, treatment of Vietnam offenders, Third World development and immigration reform, to name only a few. Justice has been the focus of many of his outside involvements. He was a charter member of the U. S. Commission on Civil Rights, created in 1957, and he chaired the commission from 1969 to 1972, when President Nixon replaced him as chairman because of his criticism of the administration's civil rights record. Father Hesburgh was a member of President Gerald Ford's Presidential Clemency Board, charged with deciding the fate of various groups of Vietnam offenders.

In 1971 he joined the board of the Overseas Development Council, a private organization supporting interests of the underdeveloped world, and chaired it until 1982. During this time, he led fund-raising efforts that averted mass starvation in Cambodia in 1979-80. Between 1979-81 he also chaired the Select Commission on Immigration and Refugee Policy, the recommendations of which became the basis of congressional reform legislation five years later. Currently, Father Hesburgh is involved in a private initiative which seeks to unite internationally known scientists and world religious leaders in condemning nuclear weapons. He helped organize a 1982 meeting in Vatican City of 58 world class scientists, from East as well as West, who called for the elimination of nuclear weapons. He subsequently brought together in Vienna leaders of six faith traditions who endorsed the view of these scientists.

Father Hesburgh stepped down from the presidency

of the University of Notre Dame June 1, 1987. He went on a year's sabbatical and returned to the campus in May 1988 as president emeritus and assumed a role in the development of two University institutes — the Notre Dame Institute for International Peace Studies and the Kellogg Institute for International Studies. He chairs the advisory committees for both institutes.

Father Hesburgh's retirement after 35 years as president ended the longest tenure among active chief executive officers of American institutions of higher education. During Hesburgh's tenure, 1952-1987, the annual operating budget went from $9.7 million to $176.6 million, the endowment from $9 million to almost $400 million, and research funding from $735,000 to $15 million. Enrollment increased from 4,979 to 9,600, faculty from 389 to 950, and degrees awarded from 1,212 to 2,500. The two major changes during the Hesburgh era were the transfer of governance from the founding religious community, the Congregation of Holy Cross, to a predominantly lay board of trustees in 1967 and the admission of women to the undergraduate program in 1972.

Chronological Table — 1917-1987

1917	**Hesburgh born-May 25th**
1917	U.S. enters World War I
1919	Peace Treaty of Paris
1920	U.S. vote to women
1925	World population estimate: 2 billion
1929	Great Depression begins
1933-1945	F.D. Roosevelt presidency
1934	**Hesburgh entered Notre Dame as a freshman**
1936	**Hesburgh sent to Gregorian University in Rome to study theology**
1939-1945	World War II
1941	U.S. enters World War II
1943	**Hesburgh ordained at Notre Dame**
1945-1953	H.S. Truman presidency
1945	**Hesburgh returned to Notre Dame to teach**
1945	First atomic bomb
1948	**Hesburgh appointed Head of Theology Department**
1949	Communists take-over China
1949	**Hesburgh named Executive Vice-President**
1950	World population estimate: 2.5 billion
1950-1953	Korean War
1953-1961	D.D. Eisenhower presidency
1951	Japanese peace treaty
1952	**Hesburgh becomes President of Notre Dame (age 35)**
1953	DNA double helix structure discovered
1954	U.S. hydrogen bomb tested
1957	U.S.S.R. launches first space satellite

1957	**Hesburgh selected as a member of the U.S. Civil Rights Commission**
1957-1970	**Hesburgh appointed member of National Science Board**
1958-1963	Pope John XXIII initiates program of change in the Catholic Church
1960	World population estimate: 3 billion
1960	U.S. Civil Rights movement
1961-1963	J.F. Kennedy presidency
1961-1973	U.S. involvement in Vietnam War
1961	U.S.S.R. and U.S. space flights — Soviets launch first man in space
1962	Cuban missile crisis
1962-1965	Vatican Council II
1963	President Kennedy assassinated
1963-1969	L.B. Johnson presidency
1963-1978	Pope Paul VI
1967	**Notre Dame's 125th Anniversary**
1967	**Governance of Notre Dame transferred to predominantly lay Board of Trustees**
1968	Student riots: U.S., France, Japan, etc.
1969-1974	R.M. Nixon presidency
1969	**Hesburgh's famous 15-minute "cease and desist" order during the campus rebellions**
1969	Successful U.S. lunar flight
1972	U.S.-U.S.S.R. Strategic Arms Limitation Treaty
1972	**Hesburgh dismissed from Civil Rights Commission by Nixon**
1972	**Notre Dame admits women to undergraduate programs**
1973	U.S. troops leave Vietnam
1973-1974	Arab Oil Embargo

1974	Resignation of President Nixon
1974-1977	G.R. Ford presidency
1974	**Hesburgh named to Presidential Clemency Board**
1977	**Hesburgh becomes U.S. ambassador and chairman of the U.S. delegation to the United Nations Conference on Science and Technology for Development**
1977	Nuclear non-proliferation treaty
1977-1981	J.E. Carter, Jr. presidency
1978	Pope John Paul II
1979	**Hesburgh appointed to Select Commission on Immigration**
1980-1981	Hostage crisis in Iran
1981-1989	R.W. Reagan presidency
1983	World population estimate: 5 billion
1985	**Institute for International Peace Studies created by Hesburgh**
1985	40th anniversary of United Nations
1986	Chernobyl Nuclear Plant disaster
1986	Space shuttle "Challenger" disaster
1986	Immigration Reform Act signed into law
1987	**Hesburgh retires as president of Notre Dame**
1987	200th anniversary of the U.S. Constitution
1987	Intermediate Nuclear Force Treaty, U.S.-U.S.S.R.

Reader's Guide

Under each quotation cited, the source of the citation is indicated in order to provide the reader with sufficient information to locate the original work in which the quotation appeared. The date of publication and page numbers are included whenever possible. Quotations are arranged chronologically under broad subject headings indicated in the table of contents, e.g., "Priesthood and Spirituality." Each quotation is numbered consecutively under each heading.

Quotations from Father Hesburgh's published works are cited in abbreviated references. The full bibliographical reference, in brackets, follows the abbreviated reference.

• *Patterns for Educational Growth* (1958) [Hesburgh, Theodore M. *Patterns for Educational Growth: Six Discourses at the University of Notre Dame.* Notre Dame, Ind: University of Notre Dame Press, 1958.]

• *More Thoughts for Our Times* (1964) [Hesburgh, Theodore M. *More Thoughts for Our Times: Three Addresses.* Thought Series, no. 2. Notre Dame, Ind: Dept. of Public Relations and Information, University of Notre Dame, 1964.]

• *Thoughts IV* (1967) [Hesburgh, Theodore M. *Thoughts IV: Five Addresses Delivered During 1967.* Thought Series, no. 4. Notre Dame, Ind.: Dept. of Public Relations and Information, University of Notre Dame, 1967.]

• *The Humane Imperative* (1974) [Hesburgh, Theodore M. *The Humane Imperative: A Challenge for the Year 2000.* New Haven: Yale University Press, 1974.]

• *The Hesburgh Papers* (1979) [Hesburgh, Theodore M. *The Hesburgh Papers: Higher Values in Higher Education.* Kansas City: Andrews and McMeel, 1979.]

• *Contemporary Issues in Higher Education*, (1985) [Hesburgh, Theodore M. "The Role of the Academy in a Nuclear Age." In *Contemporary Issues in Higher Education*, edited by John B. Bennett and J. W. Peltason, 247-66. New York: American Council on Education, 1985.]

• *Vision & Faith* (1985) [Hesburgh, Theodore M. *Vision & Faith: The Inner Life of Notre Dame*. Notre Dame, Ind.: Dept. of Public Relations and Information, University of Notre Dame, 1985.]

• *What Works for Me* (1986) ["Theodore M. Hesburgh, C.S.C." In *What Works for Me: 16 CEOs Talk About Their Careers and Commitments*, by Thomas R. Horton, 151-77. New York: Random House Business Division, 1986.]

A complete citation is given for each quote so that the reader may find the source and subsequently read the complete selection. Since many of these quotations and themes appear in more than one selection, wherever possible, the reference deemed easiest to obtain has been cited. The majority of Hesburgh's published and unpublished works are available at the Theodore M. Hesburgh Library or the Archives of the University of Notre Dame.

CHAPTER 1
Priesthood and Spirituality (PS)

Father Hesburgh, May 1977

PS 1 "The lasting works of man are those of the spirit. Without them, monuments are never better than tombs." *Patterns for Educational Growth* (1958), p. 5.

PS 2 "It is the work of wisdom to recognize the true human perfections and to order them rightly so that we do not place the goods of the body above those of the soul, those of time against those of eternity." *Patterns for Educational Growth* (1958), p. 6.

PS 3 "Our God has entered history as the living God of prophecy and promise, and we, too, enter the drama of history as men having faith in the prophecy and freedom to follow the promise." *Patterns for Educational Growth* (1958), p. 16.

PS 4 "All before Christ prepares for and anticipates His coming. All after Christ is the fulfillment of what He came to do. And all of us have a part in the doing, and in history, even though we are free to do our part well or poorly. Christ is the central focus and meaning of history in the Christian scheme of things. . . . Only Faith can see the utter uniqueness of God's great liturgy which is realized in Christ, in whom, and through whom, and with whom all creation is drawn to the service of God as a divine symphony in which all of us play a significant part." *Patterns for Educational Growth* (1958), p. 18.

PS 5 "Let us ask again and again for wisdom and courage, the light to see and the strength to do what the times demand and the richness of our heritage promises." *Patterns for Educational Growth* (1958), p. 32.

PS 6 "The actual battlefield is in the realm of ideas. No matter what the physical or material forces involved, ultimately it is ideas that will prevail, truth that will gain or lose in this struggle for the souls of men." *Patterns for Educational Growth* (1958), p. 37.

PS 7 "The crisis of our times is the almost universal divorce of the spiritual from the temporal order. The capital sin of our age is the process of secularism, which someone has aptly described as the practice of the absence of God." *Patterns for Educational Growth* (1958), p. 50.

PS 8 ". . . it may be truly concluded that, to the extent that Christ lives in us, to that extent is our work Christlike and of eternal value." *Patterns for Educational Growth* (1958), p. 52.

PS 9 "What is needed so desperately today is what Maritain calls the integral humanist, the whole man who is really at home, temporarily in time and eternally in eternity, the man who respects both orders, and neglects neither, the man who has been completely revivified by the grace of Christ, whose faith and hope and charity are able to renew, direct and revivify the things of time, and to achieve the human good in all its fullness in time while ultimately referring it to the eternal good that awaits beyond." *Patterns for Educational Growth* (1958), p. 54.

PS 10 "We can ignore the spiritual dimension of our lives, but we ignore this at our own risk, and at the price of bartering the best for that which may be good, but infinitely less important and even less satisfying in the total picture of life." Commencement Address, University of Rhode Island, 1960.

PS 11 "In respecting God and the order which He has made, we are truest to ourselves and to our common mankind." Commencement Address, University of Rhode Island, 1960.

PS 12 "Each and all of us are members of one family, at the highest level, members of the Body of Christ, Our Lord." *More Thoughts for Our Times* (1964), p. 44.

PS 13 "Commitment, compassion, consecration — wherever you go, whatever you do, these three values are sturdy companions along the way." Commencement Address, Indiana University at Bloomington, 1965.

PS 14 "In prayer and meditation we can find the tranquility and the transforming power of the presence of God. Union with God is, ultimately, the only basis on which our community with others can rest." *The Humane Imperative* (1974), p. 6.

PS 15 ". . . *Fides quaerens intellectum et intellectus quaerens fidem.* Faith seeking understanding and understanding seeking faith." *The Humane Imperative* (1974), p. 7.

PS 16 ". . . the impossible is possible with faith and hope and especially love." *The Humane Imperative* (1974), p. 16.

PS 17 "The great spiritual values — love, justice, honesty, compassion, courage, fidelity, and so many others — are what enrich a person's character and life and works. The spiritual, not the material, is the factor most important in fulfilling a person and making him or her happy. . . . Life is fundamentally tenacious, and religion makes eternal life a most tenacious hope." *The Humane Imperative* (1974), pp. 19-20.

PS 18 "To say that man is a person is to say that in the depths of his being he is more a whole than a part, and more independent than servile. It is to say that he is a minute fragment of matter that is at the same time a universe, a beggar who communicates with absolute being, mortal flesh whose value is eternal, a bit of straw into which heaven enters. . . . The value of the person, his dignity and his rights belong to the order of things naturally sacred which bear the imprint of the Father of being, and which have in Him the end of their movement." *The Humane Imperative* (1974), p. 40. (Hesburgh quoting Jacques Maritain, *Principes d'une politique humaniste* (Paris: Paul Hartmann, 1945), pp. 15-16.

PS 19 "I do not believe we should ever look back except occasionally in sorrow and occasionally in gratitude." Address, Kings College, Wilkes-Barre, Pa., 1978.

PS 20 "Humility is not just a nice virtue; it is the truth. The cemeteries of the world are full of indispensable men and women, but somehow the world goes on." *The Hesburgh Papers* (1979), p. 8.

PS 21 "We should indeed disaffiliate ourselves from any influence that is not ecumenical, that cuts us off from each other or from the world, or from the very real values that are to be derived from a wider understanding of all the social revolutions in progress." *The Hesburgh Papers* (1979), p. 59.

PS 22 "Whatever the changes in the theological perception and description of Christianity in our times, there can be no diminution of Catholic education's lifelong commitment to a concept of human life that derives its meaning, purpose, and direction from faith and hope and love of God and man." *The Hesburgh Papers* (1979), p. 83.

PS 23 "**Commitment to truth** in all its forms: the joy of ever seeking truth, the peace of finding truth everywhere, the courage of living truth always. Open-mindedness is the prelude to this commitment, intellectual honesty is its truest spirit, and purity of life is essential to both possession of the truth and commitment to what it demands of us. . . . **Commitment to what is good and excellent**. I mean here no narrowly selfish good, but that every good and noble inspiration might find in us a champion and a defender, and indeed a personification. . . . To avoid the taint of intellectual and moral mediocrity; to be willing to stand for something, even something unpopular, if it is good; to be willing to be a minority of one if needs be — this is part of the commitment." *The Hesburgh Papers* (1979), p. 97.

PS 24 "... in the broader world of man's total voyage through time to eternity, faith is not only a gracious companion, but an essential guide .... Faith begins with belief in God, he who is, the ultimate eternal source of all else that is: all truth, all goodness, all beauty, all justice, all order." *The Hesburgh Papers* (1979), p. 98.

PS 25 "Too long has there been an imagined chasm between the very real values of the physical and spiritual worlds. Faith I take to be a gift of God, but one that is amenable to rational foundations and prayerful preparation. It is rather a luminous opening on another world, that adds new personal dimensions to one's life and wider vistas to one's highest endeavors, in science or in any other field of intellectual interest." *The Hesburgh Papers* (1979), p. 99.

PS 26 "I am not sure that anyone really understands the period through which they and we are passing." *The Hesburgh Papers* (1979), p. 142.

PS 27 "We can and must do something about abortion, but it must be one of several equally horrendous problems that we are doing something about. It must not be booked as a Catholic problem either; it is a human problem." *The Hesburgh Papers* (1979), p. 186.

PS 28 "I really expect that there will be one Christian Church in the years ahead, one characterized by unity, but not by uniformity." *The Hesburgh Papers* (1979), pp. 186-87.

PS 29 "Without navigation, life today becomes irrational wandering, a journey with no homecoming, a voyage without a port of call, a story without meaning or ending. . . . We would all admit in the quiet of our consciences that justice is better than injustice, love better than hate, integrity better than dishonesty, compassion better than insensitivity, beauty better than ugliness, hope better than despair, faith better than infidelity, order better than chaos, peace better than war, life better than death, knowledge better than ignorance, and so on and on and on." *The Hesburgh Papers* (1979), p. 193.

PS 30 "Love and hate, war and peace, freedom and bondage, compassion and brutality are not merely a matter of genes. . . . At base, all human problems have a philosophical and theological dimension, if one plunges into them deeply and not superficially. Human happiness and unhappiness are not merely matters of biology, chemistry, or political science." Commencement Address, University of San Diego, 1980.

PS 31 "The strident divisions of our day, spiritual, intellectual, cultural, ethnic, political, economic, social, geographical, call for nothing less than priestly mediation if human peace and understanding are to be born and broadened in our times." Commencement Address, University of San Diego, 1980.

PS 32 "I never wanted to be anything but a priest, which is in itself a great and unearned grace. I hope to live and die a priest, nothing more, but nothing less either." Commencement Address, Immaculate Conception Seminary, 1983.

PS 33 "The priest is a man in the middle and, as a mediator, he bridges the gap between the human and the divine, between time and eternity." Commencement Address, Immaculate Conception Seminary, 1983.

PS 34 "The greatest priestly act of mediation is, of course, the Mass." Commencement Address, Immaculate Conception Seminary, 1983.

PS 35 "I confess to liking John's Gospel best of all because of his recurring emphasis on the trilogy of light, life, and love." Commencement Address, Immaculate Conception Seminary, 1983.

PS 36 "With Christ, the priest has all he needs, all the courage, all the love, all the fidelity, all the compassion, all the consecration, all the faith and hope, all the perseverence." Commencement Address, Immaculate Conception Seminary, 1983.

PS 37 "Too many priests, and other professionals, simply go to seed after a fine education. They thereby become less competent, less informed, less alive, yes, less attractive, too — all of which makes us less apostolic." Commencement Address, Immaculate Conception Seminary, 1983.

PS 38 "I pity any man, however talented, endowed, intelligent, even handsome, who tries to be a priest today without constantly saying that simplest and most efficacious of all prayers: 'Come Holy Spirit'." Commencement Address, Immaculate Conception Seminary, 1983.

PS 39 "Vision alone gives us only a visionary, in the pejorative sense of that word. But join vision and faith, and mountains begin to move." *Vision and Faith* (1985), p. 3.

PS 40 "Faith keeps the vision bright. Faith also tells us that we need help to create corporate excellence." *Vision and Faith* (1985), p. 4.

PS 41 ". . . if our commitment is obviously solid and serious and we are trying to do better, we will not have to blow a trumpet to prove it." *Vision and Faith* (1985), p. 5.

PS 42 "Searching out truth is a slow and laborious process." *Vision and Faith* (1985), p. 6.

PS 43 ". . . no humans, no problems." Eugene Burke Lecture, University of San Diego, 1985.

CHAPTER 2

Moral Values (MV)

Father Hesburgh with Pope John Paul II, November 1979

MV 1 "Next to being wrong, the worst state is to be right and not to know why, or to be right for the wrong reasons." *Dartmouth Alumni Magazine*, July, 1958, p. 16.

MV 2 "The individuality of the human person is not like the individuality of other corporal beings, because personality is not directly related to matter, man's body, but has its roots in spirit, man's immortal soul." *More Thoughts for Our Times* (1964), p. 6.

MV 3 "We live in a world of eternal verities and eternal values, surrounded by timeless traditions." *More Thoughts for Our Times* (1964), pp. 29-30.

MV 4 "The mind is always out there groping to find what is good, true, and beautiful because they are God's treasures and our patrimony." Address, Kings College, 1972.

MV 5 "To evaluate is to prefer, to discriminate, to choose, and each of these actions presupposes a sense of values." *The Humane Imperative* (1974), p. 79.

MV 6 "I know of no way of building character without adhering to a definite set of moral standards and values that make for the good life. We have cast aside too many of these standards and values, like honesty, sobriety, fidelity, justice, and magnanimity." *The Hesburgh Papers* (1979), p. 15.

MV 7 "Without a deep concern for philosophy and theology, there is always the danger that the intellectual and moral aspects of all human knowledge become detached and separate." *The Hesburgh Papers* (1979), p. 43.

MV 8 "The dignity of man is the most central moral issue of our times. One must note that every aspect of what we called 'the youth revolution' stemmed from a new perception of human dignity, a new concern to achieve more dignity and sanctity for human life, more meaning and more rights for all human beings." *The Hesburgh Papers* (1979), p. 83.

MV 9 "Today one hears all too little of intellectual values, and moral values seem to have become a lost cause in the educational process." *The Hesburgh Papers* (1979), p. 115.

MV 10 "Moral abdication or valuelessness seems to have become a sign of the times. One might well describe the illness of modern society and its schooling as *anomie*, a rootlessness." *The Hesburgh Papers* (1979), p. 116.

MV 11 "History gives a vital record of mankind's success and failure, hopes and fears, the heights and the depths of human endeavors pursued with either heroism or depravity — but always depicting real virtue or the lack of it." *The Hesburgh Papers* (1979), p. 117.

MV 12 "Whatever you value, be committed to it and let nothing distract you from this goal. The uncommitted life, like Plato's unexamined life, is not worth living." *The Hesburgh Papers* (1979), p. 124.

MV 13 "*Anomie* means restlessness, a spiritual vacuum, a lack of values, a drifting, a complete lack of conviction regarding what is important for our times in the way of priorities, values, or the ultimate meaning of life, individual or societal." *The Hesburgh Papers* (1979), p. 147.

MV 14 "We should not be afraid to seek wisdom and virtue in other cultures than our own, for greatness and goodness are humanly great and good wherever they are found." *The Hesburgh Papers* (1979), p. 193.

MV 15 "Without a sense of value, the greatest scientist and the greatest engineer in the world may be the world's greatest menace. . . ." Banquet Address, Loretto Heights College, 1982.

MV 16 "Without a sense of value and purpose the lawyer may become a clever manipulator of the law, seeking anything but justice." Banquet Address, Loretto Heights College, 1982.

MV 17 "Without values, the multinational manager may forget that foreign profit without indigenous development in that country is a formula for economic and political disaster, at home as well as abroad." Address, Loretto Heights College, 1982.

MV 18 ". . . nothing is more difficult to teach than values or the ability to evaluate — to have a growing sense of moral purpose and priority in a world often devoid of both principle and priority." Address, Loretto Heights College, 1982.

MV 19 "Our words are buttressed by our deeds, and our deeds are inspired by our convictions." *Contemporary Issues in Higher Education* (1985), p. 254.

CHAPTER 3
Human Rights (HR)

President Eisenhower appoints Father Hesburgh to the U.S. Civil Rights Commission, January 1957

HR 1 "The whole world looks anxiously to America and expects a passion for justice that will make the promise of our Constitution and Bill of Rights come true for all, here and elsewhere." Commencement Address, University of Rhode Island, 1960.

HR 2 "Man's spiritual potentialities are not well realized in an atmosphere of material stagnation, abysmal poverty, and general hopelessness." Address at a dinner honoring the National Science Board, California Institute of Technology, 1962.

HR 3 "When one man or one nation is not free, all freedom in this world is endangered." Address at a dinner honoring the National Science Board, California Institute of Technology, 1962.

HR 4 "To be concerned only on the material, social, political, economic or legal level is to forget the true roots of personal human dignity and equality, and the true eternal destiny of man." *More Thoughts for Our Times* (1964), p. 44.

HR 5 "The central idea that most challenges our nation today, indeed the world, is the idea of human equality." Commencement Address, Temple University, 1965.

HR 6 "There will be no true human equality, or equality of opportunity for all Americans, until we sense as individuals the true meaning of human dignity." Commencement Address, Temple University, 1965.

HR 7 "The most amazing aspect of the growing consciousness of human dignity is how recently it even began to blossom." *The Humane Imperative* (1974), p. 25.

HR 8 "The problem of human rights is so universal that it transcends all other problems that face humanity. . . ." *The Humane Imperative* (1974), p. 27.

HR 9 "More is required than political and civil rights to secure the dignity of human beings. We must move beyond political and civil rights and afford protection to economic and social rights as well." *The Humane Imperative* (1974), p. 33.

HR 10 "There is no more lingering problem among all mankind than prejudice. While laws can correct inequitable situations and educate while doing this, prejudice must be faced and conquered every hour of every day by every individual within his inner self." *The Humane Imperative* (1974), p. 35.

HR 11 "The same burning question remains: Are we going to stand still on basic human rights, slip back, or move forward?" *The Humane Imperative* (1974), p. 36.

HR 12 ". . . however one projects his or her hopes for the next millennium, central to every consideration will be the human person. It is the person who shares the hope and sees it realized or denied in his or her life." *The Humane Imperative* (1974), p. 38.

HR 13 "There are few sights more heartrending than human beings without food or drink. One understands, in seeing them, the premium the good Lord placed on feeding the hungry and giving drink to the thirsty." *The Humane Imperative* (1974), p. 50.

HR 14 "Hungry and undernourished people simply lack the energy to build a nation, even to live a human life or plan a better one." *The Humane Imperative* (1974), p. 56.

HR 15 "This mystery of life is what really is at the heart of our concern, because we say that it is a gift so stupendous, so magnificent, so mysterious that no one but God has any rights over it." Address at the "Respect Life" Mass, University of Notre Dame, 1975.

HR 16 "And there is no reason I know of philosophically or theologically that can say it's now, it's then, except we know that once life begins, it moves along in an inexorable path to be what it was created to be." Address at the "Respect Life" Mass, University of Notre Dame, 1975.

HR 17 "No law of man can by decree or judgement say that what is wrong in the eyes of God suddenly becomes right." Address at the "Respect Life" Mass, University of Notre Dame, 1975.

HR 18 "Curiously, those who are at the very fount of life, those who are the nurturers of life, women, are in the forefront of those proposing the legitimacy of abortion as a very sacred woman's right . . . . I happen to believe in Women's Liberation — but I do not believe in this deduction from Women's Liberation — that abortion is a fundamental right of women." Address at the "Respect Life" Mass, University of Notre Dame, 1975.

HR 19 "I think it's a terrible thing that all around this world life is degraded for people unborn and for people born and doomed to die very soon. If we really want to convince the world and our country that we have respect for life, we had better start showing respect for life and the justice that should attend the promise of life for every human being — black or white or Western or Oriental, rich or poor, young or old. . . ." Address at the "Respect Life" Mass, University of Notre Dame, 1975.

HR 20 "Human life is so depreciated and denatured in so many ways that if we want to really convince our fellow Americans that we respect the right to life then I think that we are going to have to change many of our judgments and many of our actions." Address at the "Respect Life" Mass, University of Notre Dame, 1975.

HR 21 "We must believe in and respect life deeply enough to respect it wherever it is threatened and under whatever conditions it is threatened." Address at the "Respect Life" Mass, University of Notre Dame, 1975.

HR 22 "We have often been unmindful of the fact that when one American suffers injustice, each of us and our great nation are diminished and wasted, yes, even threatened." Commencement Address, University of Denver, 1976.

HR 23 "How can three billion of the earth's inhabitants, especially those of us who live and work in universities, glory in the dawn and the high noon of human culture when one billion of our fellow human beings languish in lifelong darkness?" Address, St. Francis Xavier University, 1978.

HR 24 "In the developed world, we spend millions each year to research the few illnesses that most afflict us. But we almost entirely neglect medical research on the other tropical diseases that presently infect hundreds of millions of our brethren to the South." Address, St. Francis Xavier University, 1978.

HR 25 ". . . almost everywhere in the present world one finds majorities imposing upon minorities, the powerful abusing the weak, the affluent unmindful of the poor." Address, St. Francis Xavier University, 1978.

HR 26 "If the human condition is to improve, human beings everywhere must make common cause in using the greatest resources that God has given us, our intelligence and our freedom, and His grace, too, to transcend the human pettiness and selfishness, the national pride and religious prejudice, the cultural imperialism and color consciousness that have caused our beautiful spaceship earth to be so humanly unbeautiful and unjust and unpeaceful today." Address, St. Francis Xavier University, 1978.

HR 27 "One must say that spaceship earth looks much more beautiful from afar than it does from up close, particularly if one considers the Fourth World of human suffering and squalor." Address, Université Catholique de Louvain, 1978.

HR 28 "Openness to all is the best way of bringing all together across the gulf of deep-set misunderstandings and prejudices." Address, 75th Anniversary, Assumption College, 1979.

HR 29 "No age has seen a greater dedication to human dignity, human equality, and human development than our own. No age has had greater resources, educational, scientific, technical, and human, to do something about these deepest of human aspirations." *The Hesburgh Papers* (1979), pp. 59-60.

HR 30 "Again, we teach human dignity best by serving it where it is most likely to be disregarded, in the poor and abandoned." *The Hesburgh Papers* (1979), p. 87.

HR 31 "We must begin to repeat with Terence: nothing human is alien to me; no human insight, no human misery, no human beauty, no human knowledge, no human anguish, no human value, no human hunger. Anything less than this leads to a truncated or sterile life, a life without fullest meaning and direction and depth." *The Hesburgh Papers* (1979), p. 96.

HR 32 "If one class, or nation, or race of men is not really free, then the freedom of all men is endangered." *The Hesburgh Papers* (1979), p. 97.

HR 33 "Compassion means that you suffer with all who suffer, the hungry, the ignorant, the poor, the homeless, the hopeless, the sick, all those who suffer injustice, all who need understanding and help. . . . In modern parlance, the compassionate get with the revolution to promote human equality, human development, and to use the new science and technology in both of these causes." *The Hesburgh Papers* (1979), p. 124.

HR 34 "Only recently have we become as concerned abroad with human development as we have been with military alliances." *The Hesburgh Papers* (1979), p. 146.

CHAPTER 4

Higher Education (HR)

Father Hesburgh at Commencement, University of Notre Dame, 1977

HE 1 "You will not teach that which is most worthwhile teaching, unless somehow the truths that you have learned become the flesh and bone of your lives, incarnate in your daily living. . . . The teacher is engaged in a work of high dignity, because he is working with the elements of the soul that are eternal. . . . It matters not what the precise subject matter is, for the human mind, once opened and working, will seek the heights if a true teacher is there to guide the way." Commencement Address, Villanova University, 1958.

HE 2 "If you take yourself, your values, your world and your way of life for granted, then liberal education has not taken root in your mind and is not guiding your will." *Dartmouth Alumni Magazine*, July 1958, p. 16.

HE 3 "Our total educative process cannot lead those whom we educate to wisdom unless we begin by seeking to be wise ourselves, and to grow continually in wisdom." *Patterns for Educational Growth* (1958), p. 7.

HE 4 "The inner growth of a university depends in large measure upon the excellence of its faculty." *Patterns for Educational Growth* (1958), p. 48.

HE 5 "The task of the university today, viewed in relation to its students, is twofold. The university must somehow transmit the intellectual and moral treasures of the past to its students, and, in doing this, must also somehow integrate this heritage with the new perspectives of the present and the future." *Patterns for Educational Growth* (1958), p. 61.

HE 6 "Respect for all that is uniquely man's, spirit, mind, freedom, truth, justice, beauty — the inner dignity of the human person — this is the heritage of the West that is ours to have and to hold and to teach." *Patterns for Educational Growth* (1958), p. 62.

HE 7 "No person can be liberally educated today without a reasonable grasp of science and the great new vision of the universe, in its innermost and outermost parts, that modern science has brought us." *Patterns for Educational Growth* (1958), p. 64.

HE 8 "The fruits of a good education are these: the critical mind, the discerning spirit, the higher values, the sense of commitment, dedication and service." Commencement Luncheon Address, Columbia University, 1961.

HE 9 "Great teachers live in each one of us who have learned from them, for they have shaped in us that which is eternal." Baccalaureate Address, St. Mary's College, 1962.

HE 10 "If there is any single topic that has captured the attention of our times, it is education. Everybody today has an opinion on what is happening or should be happening to education in America." Baccalaureate Address, St. Mary's College, 1962.

HE 11 "With their total commitment to human welfare and the common good, universities and university people cannot stand by idly and watch people go hungry when the means are available to produce food in abundance." *More Thoughts for Our Times* (1964), p. 33.

HE 12 "Great educational sophistication is needed to perceive where change is essential, at what time and in what sequence, and in what direction, so that change may occur in a fruitful and orderly fashion, not just substituting a new for an old disorder." *More Thoughts for Our Times* (1964), p. 39.

HE 13 "The one great talent that characterizes a developed country is educated manpower. Recent university studies have shown that between fifty and sixty percent of the gains made in the developed countries during the past half century are the result of better educated people, more basic research, and a much more systematic use of the nation's brain power and talent." *More Thoughts for Our Times* (1964), p. 39.

HE 14 "In fact, what we need most at this junction of our history are all the qualities of the pioneer: vision, courage, confidence, a great hope inspired by faith and ever revivified by love and dedication." Address at the Special Convocation Commemorating the 125th Anniversary, University of Notre Dame, 1967.

HE 15 "The Greeks (not the fraternities!) were at their best when they insisted that (*arete*) excellence, was at the heart of human activity at its noblest, certainly at the heart of education at its civilized best." *The Humane Imperative* (1974), p. 78.

HE 16 "I think unity is basic to man's being, and unity cries out for realization in our day." Address at the Aquinas Assembly, King's College, 1972.

HE 17 "To be liberal, an education must somehow liberate a person actually to be what every person potentially is: free. . . . The first goal of a liberal education is to free a person from ignorance which fundamentally means freedom to think, clearly and logically. . . . A liberal education should also enable a person to judge, which in itself presupposes the ability to evaluate: to prefer this to that, to say this is good and that bad, or at least this is better than that. . . . Liberal education should also enable a person to situate himself or herself within a given culture, religion, race, sex, and hopefully, to appreciate what is valuable in the given situation, even as simple an evaluation as 'black is beautiful'. . . . Liberal education, by all of these value-laden processes, should confer a sense of peace, confidence and assurance on the person thus educated and liberate him or her from the adriftness that characterizes so many in an age of anomie." *The Humane Imperative* (1974), p. 79.

HE 18 "Lastly, a liberal education should enable a person to humanize everything that he or she touches in life, which is to say that one is enabled not only to evaluate what one is or does, but that, in addition, one adds value consciously to relationships that might otherwise be banal or superficial or meaningless: relations to God, to one's fellow men, to one's wife or husband or children, to one's associates, one's neighborhood, one's country and world." *The Humane Imperative* (1974), pp. 79-80.

HE 19 "Music and art purvey a sense of beauty seen or heard, a value to be preferred to ugliness or cacophony." *The Humane Imperative* (1974), p. 80.

HE 20 "Value is simply central to all that is liberalizing in liberal education. Without value, it would be impossible to visualize liberal education as all that is good, in both the intellectual and the moral order of human development and liberation." *The Humane Imperative* (1974), p. 81.

HE 21 "Values are exemplified better than they are taught, which is to say that they are taught better by exemplification than by words." *The Humane Imperative* (1974), p. 82.

HE 22 "In a word, people deserve to be treated with humane sensitivity, even when all our inclinations push us toward brusque rejection, not only of their proposals, but also of themselves, as persons." *The Hesburgh Papers* (1979), p. 9.

HE 23 "It is mainly through liberal education that one learns how to think clearly, logically, beautifully; how to express oneself; how to learn continually in a wide variety of ways; how to evaluate ideas and ideals; how to appreciate where mankind has been and is going." *The Hesburgh Papers* (1979), pp. 29-30.

HE 24 "The university is the only institution in modern society that is largely supported by society and yet claims a unique autonomy to criticize the very society that once gave it birth and now gives it financial support." *The Hesburgh Papers* (1979), p. 31.

HE 25 "A university is a wonderful home if one wishes to be intellectually alive, free, and ever open to further growth in mind and spirit." *The Hesburgh Papers* (1979), p. 33.

HE 26 ". . . the university is the place where young people come of age — an often unruly process — places where the really important problems are freely discussed with all manner of solutions proposed, places where all the burning issues of the day are ventilated, even with hurricane winds at times . . . . The best and only traditional authority in the university is intellectual competence: this is the coin of the realm." *The Hesburgh Papers* (1979), p. 41.

HE 27 " As Cardinal Newman said so well: 'Great minds need elbow room, not indeed in the domain of faith, but of thought. And so indeed do lesser minds and all minds' ". *The Hesburgh Papers* (1979), p. 42.

HE 28 "Any university should be a place where all the relevant questions are asked and where answers are elaborated in an atmosphere of freedom and responsible inquiry, where the young learn the great power of ideas and ideals, where the values of justice and charity, truth and beauty, are both taught and exemplified by the faculty, and where both faculty and students together are seized by a deep compassion for the anguishes of mankind in our day and committed to proffer a helping hand, wherever possible, in every aspect of man's material, intellectual, and cultural development." *The Hesburgh Papers* (1979), pp. 42-43.

HE 29 "Both philosophy and theology are concerned with the ultimate questions, both bear uniquely on the nature and destiny of man, and all human intellectual questions, if pursued far enough, reveal their philosophical and theological dimension of meaning and relevance." *The Hesburgh Papers* (1979), p. 43.

HE 30 "At the heart of our specific endeavor are two great educational qualities: commitment and freedom. Have no fear of commitment as long as it is intelligent and deeply believes on real evidence the truth of those great Christian values to which we are committed. Have no fear of freedom either. It is the context within which commitment grows, deepens and is enriched, as we freely seek a greater dimension of understanding, a broader unity within the total reality we know, and a better expression of all these values that will speak to the heart of modern humanity in words that they, too, will understand and appreciate." *The Hesburgh Papers* (1979), p. 61.

HE 31 "Academic freedom, like all freedom, is grounded ultimately in the nature of man and of society and of the development of knowledge and intelligence. Man's greatest genius and dignity, as well as his last best hope, are in his intellect and in his search for truth." *The Hesburgh Papers* (1979), p. 64.

HE 32 "If the university is not to amuse or distract, rather than to educate its students, it must resist a superficial *nowness* of concern, a relevancy of today that passes all too quickly with tomorrow, a relevancy that will all too soon be a monumental irrelevancy." *The Hesburgh Papers* (1979), p. 76.

HE 33 "If our lives in education have any meaning or significance, it will be in our reading the signs of the times and in educating the young of our times in the visions and values that will civilize and make for reasonable human progress and lasting peace on earth." *The Hesburgh Papers* (1979), p. 83.

HE 34 "What is really needed today is not exclusivity of knowledge, but a deeper unity of all knowledge, past, present, and yet to come." *The Hesburgh Papers* (1979), p. 96.

HE 35 "Learning research is sterile if it is never related to the third of mankind that is illiterate, either actually or functionally." *The Hesburgh Papers* (1979), p. 110.

HE 36 "There is no way of learning values apart from the liberal arts and sciences. Learning values has always been a difficult task. Without liberal education, it is an impossible task." *The Hesburgh Papers* (1979), p. 113.

HE 37 "Liberal education, by all of these value-laden processes, should confer a sense of peace, confidence, and assurance on the person thus educated and liberate him or her from the adriftness that characterizes so many in an age of anomie." *The Hesburgh Papers* (1979), p. 116.

HE 38 "Value is simply central to all that is liberalizing in liberal education. . . . I have long believed that a Christian university is worthless in our day unless it conveys to all who study within it a deep sense of the dignity of the human person. . . ." *The Hesburgh Papers* (1979), p. 118.

HE 39 "There is nothing automatic about the liberal education tradition. It can die if not fostered. And if it does die, the values that sustain an individual and a nation are likely to die with it." *The Hesburgh Papers* (1979), p. 119.

HE 40 "If one must fault presidents and chancellors among others, and we must, it would have to be for lack of moral leadership, not just in time of crisis, but more consistently in earlier and peaceful times. We too often were blind to the moral implications of unbridled educational growth that was certainly spectacular but questionably educational. . . . Once we washed our hands of any moral concern for all that was happening in our academic communities, we reaped the harvest of a disintegrating community. I grant that the great wisdom and courage required for moral leadership are not common qualities among men and women, but then neither are college or university presidencies common tasks." *The Hesburgh Papers* (1979), p. 155.

HE 41 "I have a strong belief, nurtured no doubt by my own prejudices, that the central person in exercising moral leadership for the life and prosperity of any academic institution must be its president. He must, first and foremost, speak for the priorities that really count in academia." *The Hesburgh Papers* (1979), p. 156.

HE 42 "When members of a college or university stop caring about each other or their institution, or become unclear about personal or institutional goals, then community ceases to be and chaos results. . . . When a faculty and a student body know that their president really cares about them, they will follow him to the heights, even out of the depths." *The Hesburgh Papers* (1979), p. 157.

HE 43 "Leadership may be most important at the presidential level, but it is absolutely essential at every level — trustees, faculty, administrators, students, and alumni — if the community is going to be equal to the task that lies ahead for each college and university and for the total enterprise of higher education in America." *The Hesburgh Papers* (1979), p. 158.

HE 44 "The university cannot cure all our ills today, but it can make a valiant beginning by bringing all its intellectual and moral powers to bear upon them: all the idealism and generosity of its young people, all the wisdom and intelligence of its oldsters, all the expertise and competence of those who are in their middle years." *The Hesburgh Papers* (1979), p. 165.

HE 45 "Universities, like countries, can be equally destroyed from inside or from outside." *The Hesburgh Papers* (1979), p. 170.

HE 46 "When moral persuasion and academic sanctions fail to deter those who show open contempt for the lifestyle and self-declared values of the university community, there should be no hesitation to invoke whatever outside assistance is necessary to preserve the university and its values." *The Hesburgh Papers* (1979), p. 171.

HE 47 "A rebirth of great academic, civic and political leadership, a sharing of some of these youthful ideals and dreams (impossible or not) would be good for our universities and good for America too." *The Hesburgh Papers* (1979), p. 172.

HE 48 "The human spirit, ironically, gains such freedom as is accessible by the route of interdiction; by the acceptance of limits; by the disciplines of social and institutional involvement." *The Hesburgh Papers* (1979), p. 179.

HE 49 "Prophecy here brings a dire warning — if we do not cherish quality of education and the highest educational standards, we will have given equal access to that which is really not worth having, because without high quality, education is a counterfeit and a fraud." *The Hesburgh Papers* (1979), p. 192.

HE 50 ". . . one of the most important roles of higher education today is not just to educate students to academic excellence and professional competence, although we must do this first and foremost, but also to give them the vision and the practice of serving the nation's needy." Commencement Address, Johns Hopkins University, 1980.

HE 51 "Liberal education is perhaps best described as the education which liberates a person to be truly human. . . . I think we are at our best when we are most splendidly human — when our young men and young women are liberated through education from that dark side of humanity that is most fundamentally called evil. . . . Literature enlarges the human experience to live a thousand lives and to learn from each one of them. . . . Thinking clearly is essential to expressing oneself clearly." Address, Loretto Heights College, 1982.

HE 52 "The purpose of learning is to save the soul and enlarge the mind." Address at the Annual Meeting of the Association of Catholic Colleges and Universities, Washington, D.C., 1983.

HE 53 "Athletes represent the college or university in the national limelight for four or five years and are then casually discarded without receiving the greatest gift that these institutions were created to transmit — a good education and the values that this education implies for one's whole life." Remarks at the Heisman Memorial Trophy Award Dinner, New York, N.Y., 1987.

Father Hesburgh giving the homily during a Mass for the World Hunger Coalition, University of Notre Dame, 1975

HND 1 "What are the challenges of the spirit that face our civilization, our country, and our University today? Certainly, a prime challenge is the need for wisdom, not merely the pragmatic prudence of day-by-day decisions, but the age-old Christian wisdom that understands the whole pattern of creation and man's place in this pattern." *Patterns for Educational Growth* (1958), p. 5.

HND 2 "We cannot have too much wisdom, any more than we can have too much life or holiness." *Patterns for Educational Growth* (1958), p. 7.

HND 3 "May God, the Holy Spirit, fill all of us with wisdom today and through the year, and may Notre Dame, the Mother of God and the seat of wisdom, be our beacon along the way." *Patterns for Educational Growth* (1958), p. 9.

HND 4 "There is no human event, no human progress in knowledge, science, or art that cannot be consecrated to a higher service, now that God has literally become man and dwelt amongst us." *Patterns for Educational Growth* (1958), p. 18.

HND 5 "Our prime concern must be to offer a worthy gift to the service of God and man. Certainly, we should not offer as our part in this divine symphony of all creation, the sour notes of intellectual mediocrity or educational complacency." *Patterns for Educational Growth* (1958), pp. 18-19.

HND 6 "Our aim must be a Christian humanism born of the Incarnation of the Son of God, a humanism embracing all the wide dimensions of the world and the human spirit, a humanism that is adequate to the designs of God for Notre Dame, named and consecrated as we are to the honor of her who is most perfectly, most beautifully, most gracefully, and most wisely human." *Patterns for Educational Growth* (1958), p. 19.

HND 7 "Excellence as such has no direct relation to size or age." *Patterns for Educational Growth* (1958), p. 23.

HND 8 "The university prospers when men are willing to stand firmly for the value of things intellectual, to devote themselves wholeheartedly to study and learning and teaching that the human intellect may 'become richer and stronger, broader in appreciation and sympathy, more firm in judgement, more sure in action . . . to gain at last some measure of wisdom, some vision of truth, some understanding of the Will of God.' " *Patterns for Educational Growth* (1958), p. 25.

HND 9 "Our own American past gives us much to be thankful for. Notre Dame's own history is a thrilling account of sacrifice, devotion, and sheer pioneering doggedness that brought this University from a low grade grammar school to what it is today." *Patterns for Educational Growth* (1958), p. 30.

HND 10 "The world is poorer today for secularism, and will be poorer still if the work of incarnation does not take root in the lives of our laymen. I know of no place where this new breath of divine life could more effectively grow and multiply than here at Notre Dame. . . . Our work of education is in the world, but never completely of the world." *Patterns for Educational Growth* (1958), p. 54.

HND 11 "The mind of Christ and the will of Christ are models for teacher and student alike, a pattern for growth in wisdom and age and grace, a prototype towards which all Catholic education must strive." Commencement Address, Villanova University, 1958.

HND 12 "Education is most Catholic when in curiosity and wonderment it embraces all that is, the totality of creation, both spirit and matter." Baccalaureate Address, St. Mary's College, 1962.

HND 13 "If Catholic education leaves us with one deep conviction it should be this: that only by living daily with Christ, in the state of grace, can we make the cross of daily tasks become pure gold, of eternal value." Commencement Address, Rosary College, 1963.

HND 14 "If Catholic higher education does not inspire young people to dare, to be different, to give of themselves, to court insecurity for a higher end, then it will have no serious reason to survive." Commencement Address, Providence College, 1968.

HND 15 "All of the problems that seize the modern world — war and peace and disarmament, terrorism and refugees, drugs and disease, health and food and development, population and pollution — all of these problems have an overriding moral dimension that can most conveniently be discussed without embarrassment, in fact, with enthusiasm, in a Catholic institution of higher learning." Address at the 75th Anniversary, Assumption College, 1979.

HND 16 "In a true Catholic university, all the doors should be open, and the windows, too. We should listen to everyone and be ready to discuss anything with anyone." Address at the 75th Anniversary, Assumption College, 1979.

HND 17 "A great Catholic university must begin by being a great university that is also Catholic." *The Hesburgh Papers* (1979), p. 42.

HND 18 "Catholic means universal and the university, as Catholic, must be universal in a double sense: first, it must emphasize the centrality of philosophy and, especially, theology among its intellectual concerns, not just to fill a large gap in the total fabric of knowledge as represented in most modern university curricula. Rather, theology in the Catholic university must be engaged on the highest level of intellectual inquiry so that it may be in living dialogue with all the other disciplines in the university." *The Hesburgh Papers* (1979), p. 43.

HND 19 "At Notre Dame, as in all universities, commitment to be meaningful must be personal rather than institutional, a thing of personal free conviction rather than institutional rhetoric." *The Hesburgh Papers* (1979), p. 44.

HND 20 "Whatever the personal faith of our variegated faculty and student body, I have sensed that we are united in believing that intellectual virtues and moral values are important to life and to this institution." *The Hesburgh Papers* (1979), pp. 44-45.

HND 21 "I take it that our total community commitment is to wisdom, which is something more than knowledge and much akin to goodness and beauty when it radiates throughout a human person." *The Hesburgh Papers* (1979), p. 45.

HND 22 "To be such a mediator, the Catholic university, as universal, must have a foot and an interest in both worlds, to understand each, to encompass each in its total community and to build a bridge of understanding and love. Here the name of the game is peace, not conflict." *The Hesburgh Papers* (1979), pp. 46-47.

HND 23 "Somehow, the Notre Dame community should reflect profoundly, and with unashamed commitment, its belief in the existence of God and in God's total revelation to man, especially the Christian message. . . ." *The Hesburgh Papers* (1979), p. 45.

HND 24 ". . . the Catholic university must be a crossroads where all the intellectual and moral currents of our times meet and are thoughtfully considered." *The Hesburgh Papers* (1979), p. 47.

HND 25 "The Catholic university today must be a university in the full modern sense of the word, with a strong commitment to and concern for academic excellence." *The Hesburgh Papers* (1979), p. 64. (Quoting the 1967 Land O'Lakes Statement).

HND 26 "Professionalism and competence are the coin of this realm. Again, there is no first-class institution of higher learning where this is not the order of the day." *The Hesburgh Papers* (1979), p. 72.

HND 27 "We should involve students in every legitimate way to the extent that they are willing to assume responsibility, as well as to assert their rights." *The Hesburgh Papers* (1979), p. 78.

HND 28 "While I personally have been greatly concerned in turning out graduates who are intellectually competent, I am even more concerned in turning out students who are deeply compassionate." *The Hesburgh Papers* (1979), p. 79.

HND 29 "Maybe instead of worrying about the changes ahead of us, we should rather decide which changes are needed and overdue, and effect them with vision, vitality, enthusiasm, and verve." *The Hesburgh Papers* (1979), p. 80.

HND 30 "We must now endow students not only with competence, but also with the compassion and commitment to use their competence in the interest of the less fortunate." *The Hesburgh Papers* (1979), p. 84.

HND 31 "I have long believed that a Christian university is worthless in our day unless it conveys to all who study within it a deep sense of the dignity of the human person, his nature and high destiny, his opportunities for seeking justice in a very unjust world, his inherent nobility so needing to be realized, for one's self and for others, whatever the obstacles." *The Hesburgh Papers* (1979), pp. 118-19.

HND 32 ". . . all those engaged in education today must look to themselves first, to their moral commitments, to their lives, and to their own values, which, for better or worse, will be reflected in the lives and attitudes of those they seek to educate." *The Hesburgh Papers* (1979), p. 119.

HND 33 "One bit of advice our most active students needed to hear from faculty was that action is most fruitful when it is backed up, not by emotion, or mass hysteria, or noise, or violence, but by intelligent and competent leadership, which is the fruit of a good education that is taken seriously during the years when it is available." *The Hesburgh Papers* (1979), pp. 135-36.

HND 34 "They (students) believe in the virtue of compassion for mankind, so often the victim of man's inhumanity to man. They sense that law and order are not possible in a world, or in a nation, or in a university in which there is not a deep concern for justice and equality and the development of a better world." *The Hesburgh Papers* (1979), pp. 146-47.

HND 35 "Beyond being a house of the intellect, the Catholic university must also be the intellect searching for faith and values and deeper meaning, faith searching for greater understanding and grace, closed to none, open to all, seated in time, yearning for eternity, a pilgrim institution with a pilgrim's faith and hope and love." Commencement Address, University of San Diego, 1980.

HND 36 "I regret saying this, but we still have a long way to go, not as far as in 1952, but still a long way because we are now competing with the few best universities in the land." Address to Faculty, University of Notre Dame, 1985.

HND 37 "Quality must be born and nurtured; it must grow and mature. It must be achieved step-by-step, day-by-day, with persistence, fidelity and dogged determination." Address to Faculty, University of Notre Dame, 1985.

HND 38 ". . . if a university is not an oasis of quality in a sea of mediocrity, it does not deserve the name university." Address to Faculty, University of Notre Dame, 1985.

HND 39 "I wanted Notre Dame to be a great university and also to be a great Catholic university. The first is easier to do than the second, for there are many great universities; but there has not been, since the Middle Ages, a great Catholic university." Quoted from *"What Works for Me"* by Thomas Horton (1986), p. 176.

HND 40 "How does one describe, for those who haven't spent years here, how special this place is?" Valedictory to Alumni and Friends, University of Notre Dame, 1987.

HND 41 "If we are faithful to our Catholic heritage and our dedication to Our Lady in this place, the future may well make the past look dull and uneventful." Valedictory to Alumni and Friends, University of Notre Dame, 1987.

HND 42 "I leave this university, as Sorin did on that first snowy, frozen November founding day in 1842, in the hands of Notre Dame, Our Lady." Valedictory to Alumni and Friends, University of Notre Dame, 1987.

Father Hesburgh offering Mass at the dedication of the Clarke Memorial on the campus of the University of Notre Dame, October 1986

P 1 "... modern man stands or cowers beneath a mushroom cloud. He has created it and in a sense it symbolizes all his efforts of self-destruction across all the ages. Yet he seeks a deeper meaning. Life cannot be simply negation and despair, so he seeks a faith: in God, in God's Word, in God Incarnate in Christ our Lord, in suffering and resurrection, in life eternal. These are the only realities that keep man today from the ultimate despair, suicide, either personal or global." *Thoughts IV* (1967), p. 12.

P 2 "If there is to be more lasting peace among the crew members of spaceship earth, the first and greatest prerequisite at this historical moment is justice, a more equitable sharing and use of the total life resources available." Address, St. Francis Xavier University, 1978.

P 3 "If religious persons are committed profoundly to one simple reality all around the world, it must be to peace. . . . Without justice, especially to the poor, the homeless and the hopeless, there will be no peace." Address at the Lincoln Memorial, Washington, D.C., 1979.

P 4 "Take the issue of war and peace. It is certainly in our tradition that violent solutions are idiotic approaches to the resolution of human problems, that they are only productive of widows and orphans, destruction and ruin, degradation, not civilization. Our educational efforts should be sensitive to every endeavor to foster peace and nonviolence as the greatest values for humans in a world given over to violence, destruction, and war." *The Hesburgh Papers* (1979), p. 84.

P 5 "The widespread ignorance of Catholics in America regarding traditional Catholic and Christian opposition to military conscription has once again intensified within me the shattering realization that on the primordial moral questions regarding peace in the family of nations, millions of Catholics are morally and theologically illiterate." *The Hesburgh Papers* (1979), p. 85.

P 6 "No matter how quickly the world's population multiplies, all the earth's people can now be destroyed in a matter of seconds and the earth itself made uninhabitable." *The Hesburgh Papers* (1979), pp. 123-24.

P 7 "What I am suggesting is that each human being be given the option of dual citizenship. All are, in fact, citizens of the country in which they were born. Why not give everyone the additional option, in this largely interdependent world, of opting for dual citizenship — world citizenship, in addition to national citizenship? Everyone opting for world citizenship would have to produce some evidence of his dedication to world justice and peace, some perception of the interdependence of all mankind on spaceship earth today. I think all of us will be surprised to see how many of the younger generation will opt for dual citizenship and work for global justice." *The Hesburgh Papers* (1979), p. 206.

P 8 "If we do not learn and teach our students how to cope with this primordial nuclear problem, we need not worry about all the others. After total nuclear conflagration, all human problems are moot." *Contemporary Issues in Higher Education* (1985), p. 255.

P 9 "Never before has humankind — mostly mankind — had in their hands the power to destroy the total work of creation, fourteen times over, in a few minutes, even accidentally. . . . Limited or winnable nuclear war is a most foolish illusion." *Contemporary Issues in Higher Education* (1985), p. 257.

P 10 "There is no truth about the world and humankind today that does not become darkened in the shadow of the thermonuclear mushroom and nuclear winter." *Contemporary Issues in Higher Education* (1985), p. 261.

CHAPTER 7

Science and Technology (ST)

A candid photograph of Father Hesburgh in his office, 1973

ST 1 "We are told that we are fortunate people to be living in this age of science. People of other ages had to be satisfied with God, or truth, or beauty, or the good, but we, thanks to the new technology, have science, and with it, the blessings of supersonic speed for aimless travelers, electronic communication devices for thoughtless speakers, and H-bombs for those millions whose life span science has increased by seven years and six months." Address at the dedication of Science Hall, St. Mary's College, 1955.

ST 2 "What is saddest in the picture of modern science is the fact that it is unrelated to the greater divine and human realities that supersede it in importance and scope, that alone can give science human meaning and purpose." Address at the dedication of Science Hall, St. Mary's College, 1955.

ST 3 ". . . science can make man comfortable, but only wisdom can make man happy." Address at the President's Dinner, University of Notre Dame, 1957.

ST 4 "Science is most truly valued when it is viewed in the total perspective of man's life and destiny, not as an exclusive blessing." *Patterns for Educational Growth* (1958), p. 60.

ST 5 "At this present juncture of history, our greatest challenge and opportunity is to understand both the vital importance of our heritage and the growing importance of science, so that working together, instead of at cross purposes, our heritage may be enriched and science may become a fruitful instrument of man, not his master or destroyer." *Patterns for Educational Growth* (1958), p. 64.

ST 6 "Science is power, and power needs direction to be meaningful. . . . Science of itself cannot know God, or the nature of man, cannot establish justice, define morality, constitute culture or write poetry." *Patterns for Educational Growth* (1958), p. 65.

ST 7 "One of the most popular endeavors today is the quest for goals, personal, national, international, and, even to some extent, interplanetary." Commencement Address, University of Rhode Island, 1960.

ST 8 ". . . science and technology are morally neutral, ready and available to serve any goal men choose, good or evil." Address at a dinner honoring the National Science Board, California Institute of Technology, 1962.

ST 9 "I submit to you that what really has impact on the earth's people, outside of America, is that thanks to science and technology, we are wealthy while they are poor, we are healthy while they are diseased, we live in palaces compared to their shacks, we are well fed while they are hungry, we are educated while they are ignorant, in sum, we have the good life while they have only frustrated hopes. . . . Maybe it's time for scientists and engineers to become philosophers and theologians, too, that they might question the moral impact of their work on the world of man in which they live. . . . It really makes little practical difference if scientists and engineers in the Soviet realm are forced to dedicate their lives to utterly materialistic ends, and ours are seduced to do likewise, by financial support, by prestigious appointments, or by the wave of our present affluent culture and material preoccupations." Address at a dinner honoring the National Science Board, California Institute of Technology, 1962.

ST 10 "Science and technology are champions of freedom because they present us with new and most efficacious means of liberating the people of the less-developed countries from their ancient and traditional servitudes of ignorance, illness, malnutrition, lack of adequate shelter and clothing." *More Thoughts for our Times* (1964), p. 31.

ST 11 ". . . we continue to produce scientists and engineers who are technically competent as scientists and engineers, but often completely innocent of the values that give human life larger meaning. Should we then be surprised if there are 80 engineers working for international development and 8,000 for the space agency?" *More Thoughts for Our Times* (1964), p. 57.

ST 12 "Two decades ago, President Kennedy announced that in a decade we would put men on the moon and return them safely to earth. I believe that the most spectacular result of this successful endeavor was not the close up view of the moon, but the startling view of the earth from afar. For the first time in the history of mankind, we humans saw what our earth looks like from the moon, a beautiful satellite, blue, brown, and flecked with white clouds, spinning in the black void of space." Address, St. Francis Xavier University, 1978.

ST 13 "Never before in the history of mankind could we have even dreamed of creating a much better world for so many people: modern science and technology have given us a new key to the future. Unfortunately, we have more readily used this new knowledge and power for destructive or trivial purposes." Address, Université Catholique de Louvain, 1978.

ST 14 "The trivial use of science and technology may mean a great personal profit to the scientist or engineer; the noble is rarely profitable." *The Hesburgh Papers* (1979), p. 93.

ST 15 "In a free world, it is man, the scientist or engineer, who makes the choice of goals for science and technology in our day." *The Hesburgh Papers* (1979), p. 94.

ST 16 "Science and technology cannot have their true human meaning and direction without reference to this total world of the human spirit." *The Hesburgh Papers* (1979), pp. 95-96.

ST 17 "It is meaningless and futile . . . to labor for better communications without being interested and concerned about what is being communicated, to make abundance of food available in one corner of the world for storage while countless millions go hungry, to make quantum advances in the speed of transportation without ever asking yourselves: why am I here and where am I going?" *The Hesburgh Papers* (1979), p. 96.

ST 18 "Faith is not an easy virtue for scientists and engineers, who in their own professions instinctively take nothing on faith. But in the broader world of man's total voyage through time to eternity, faith is not only a gracious companion, but an essential guide." *The Hesburgh Papers* (1979), p. 98.

ST 19 "Much would be gained, I believe, if the scientists and engineers in our day were men of faith as well as men of science." *The Hesburgh Papers* (1979), p. 99.

ST 20 "Social scientists are forfeiting their highest privilege when they approach man in the same manner as a physicist studying the activity of high energy particles or a chemist investigating electron paramagnetic resonance." *The Hesburgh Papers* (1979), p. 110.

ST 21 "Man lives and grows daily on moral rather than mathematical certitudes." *The Hesburgh Papers* (1979), p. 110.

ST 22 "What I am saying, hopefully, loudly, and clearly, is that concern on the part of the social scientist as a person should in some measure be followed by commitment." *The Hesburgh Papers* (1979), p. 111.

ST 23 "The physical sciences are a symphony of world order, so often unsuccessfully sought by law, but already achieved by creation, a model challenging man's freedom and creativity. The social sciences show man at work, theoretically and practically, creating his world. Too often, social scientists in their quest for a physical scientist's objectivity underrate the influence of freedom — for good or for evil." *The Hesburgh Papers* (1979), p. 117.

ST 24 "One might ask where the physical sciences liberate, but even here, the bursting knowledge of the physical sciences is really power to liberate mankind: from hunger, from ignorance and superstition, from grinding poverty and homelessness, all of the conditions that have made millions of persons less than human. But the price of this liberation is value: the value to use the power of science for the humanization rather than the destruction of mankind." *The Hesburgh Papers* (1979), p. 118.

ST 25 "Science cannot substitute for culture, nor the body for the soul in the course of development." *The Hesburgh Papers* (1979), p. 123.

ST 26 "I doubt that we will have heard from other intelligent beings in the universe by the year 2000, although I have no doubt that they are there." *The Hesburgh Papers* (1979), p. 191.

ST 27 "Human ingenuity in the face of crisis has been one of mankind's greatest glories." *The Hesburgh Papers* (1979) p. 201.

ST 28 "The world itself has successively passed through a whole series of intellectual revolutions, renaissance, reformation, the creations of nationalism, industrialization, and, more lately, the cold rationalism of science, including social science, and technology. We have been both thrilled and threatened by the advent of atomic power, the computer, and the space age." Address, Assumption College, 1979.

ST 29 "Values do not emerge from science and technology." Commencement Address, University of San Diego, 1980.

ST 30 "The world is in many ways a technological wasteland today, not because science and technology, or the scientific method are bad, but because they tell us nothing about values or the meaning of life." Commencement Address, University of Seattle, 1981.

ST 31 "Every civilization needs a kind of challenge. Space exploration is just such a challenge. . . . We are the first generation of human beings who have breached the bounds of earth." Address to the Business-Higher Education Forum, University of Notre Dame, 1985.

CHAPTER 8

Service (S)

Doctor Tom Dooley, one of Father Hesburgh's models for commitment, compassion, and consecration, with three children in Southeast Asia

S 1 "We are not independent of each other: we share the same divine life, that of Christ, Our Head. In serving others, we serve Christ, and if we should despise another, we despise Christ." *Patterns for Educational Growth* (1958), p. 51.

S 2 "We in America will sleep uneasily on our Beautyrest mattresses if we remember that a third of mankind has gone to bed hungry." *Dartmouth Alumni Magazine*, July, 1958, p. 18.

S 3 ". . . no great society or great civilization was ever built by the uncommitted, those who played it cool." Commencement Address, University of Illinois at Urbana, 1966.

S 4 "Over the years, I have stood at the graveside of many of my university colleagues and have contemplated the quiet nobility of their lives, so totally and unselfishly given to the higher education of young men and women. Some day, some of my lifelong associates will stand at my graveside. At that time, I would be greatly honored if they should say, 'Well, we worked together for a long time. We didn't always agree, but that never bothered our friendship or our forward march. At least, he was fair and tried to make the place better. Now he can rest in peace.'" *The Hesburgh Papers* (1979), p. 16.

S 5 "How hollow our words without our actions. . . . The proudest boast I can make for our students is that the vast majority of them are involved in some kind of social action, helping those less fortunate, whatever their need." *The Hesburgh Papers* (1979), p. 86.

S 6 "Our Lord once said that we must lose our lives to gain them. The compassionate lose themselves in helping others, but in a real sense, they are the only moderns who really learn who they are, what they cherish, what makes their lives rich beyond accounting." *The Hesburgh Papers* (1979), p. 124.

S 7 "Consecration means that we take gifts we have from God and give them back in service." *The Hesburgh Papers* (1979), p. 125.

S 8 "The world always needs energy, imagination, concern, idealism, dedication, commitment, service." *The Hesburgh Papers* (1979), p. 134.

S 9 "Compassion has a quiet way of service." *The Hesburgh Papers* (1979), p. 165.

S 10 "Take the volunteer associations and activities out of just one life and there is practically nothing left." Commencement Address, Rensselaer Polytechnic Institute, 1980.

S 11 "Despite our history of voluntarism . . . I sense that today, there is a tendency to say 'let the government do it.' And I say to you . . . that when the government does it, the doing is always more costly . . . less free . . . more complicated, and generally less productive and effective." Commencement Address, Rensselaer Polytechnic Institute, 1980.

S 12 "Voluntarism in its many, many faceted manifestations in our land is, I believe, America uniquely at its best." Commencement Address, Rensselaer Polytechnic Institute, 1980.

S 13 "We take voluntarism so much for granted in America that its importance is really not appreciated until we compare our way of life to that in countries where everything is of the state, by the state, and for the state — even citizens and their rights." Address at the 104th Anniversary Commemoration, Johns Hopkins University, 1980.

S 14 "To the extent that we say, 'let the government do it,' we are bartering away our freedom and generally paying for inefficiency and involuntary servitude, akin to that suffered in Socialist states." Address at the 104th Anniversary Commemoration, Johns Hopkins University, 1980.

S 15 ". . . there is a great satisfaction in finding some solutions to difficult social problems — maybe more than playing golf or bridge. . . ." Commencement Address, University of Michigan, 1981.

Father Hesburgh and honorary degree recipient President Jimmy Carter at the Notre Dame Commencement Exercises of 1972

L 1 "The means of liberating mankind are not wanting, only the people with the dedication and compassion to use the means and to demonstrate that, with new leadership from the university world, science and technology need not be the destroyer, but the new liberators of mankind." *More Thoughts for Our Times* (1964), p. 34.

L 2 "Every human group cedes to strong, intelligent, and courageous leadership." Remarks, University of Montreal, 1965.

L 3 "I heard a joke the other day about a university president who died and went to hell and was there four days before he noticed the difference." Address to the National Catholic Educational Association, Detroit, 1969.

L 4 "Be sure that all those who help you achieve your vision receive a large share of the credit. . . . Never pass off on your associates all the dirty work of administration." *The Hesburgh Papers* (1979), p. 8.

L 5 "Those presidents who are generally unsuccessful fail often from lack of humanity." *The Hesburgh Papers* (1979), p. 9.

L 6 "The greatest gift a president can give his students is the example of his life." *The Hesburgh Papers* (1979), p. 13.

L 7 "The times call for vision and leadership to an extraordinary degree, and hope as well. The French have a saying that 'fear is a poor counselor.' I suppose that the obverse of that is a call to each of us to use our freedom with courage and, hopefully, with wisdom." *The Hesburgh Papers* (1979), p. 67.

L 8 "I grant as well that, in its early stages, disintegration of a community is almost imperceptible to all but the very wisest and that, as disintegration brings on a crisis of legitimacy and credibility, superhuman courage and charisma are needed to recreate what has been largely lost." *The Hesburgh Papers* (1979), p. 155.

L 9 "There is no magic formula for presidential leadership. Each president must establish his own credibility. He will do this best by the goals which shine through his own life and activities. . . . The president, above all other members in the community, must portray respect for the mind and its special values, for true learning and culture, for humanity and humane concerns, for academic freedom, for justice and equality, in all that the university or college touches, especially the lives of its students, faculty, and alumni." *The Hesburgh Papers* (1979), p. 156.

L 10 "... I must insist that the president communicates best by what he is and what he does with his own life." *The Hesburgh Papers* (1979), pp. 156-57.

L 11 "The mystique of leadership, be it educational, political, religious, commercial, or whatever, is next to impossible to describe, but wherever it exists, morale flourishes, people pull together towards common goals, spirits soar, order is maintained not as an end in itself, but as a means to move forward together. Such leadership always has a moral as well as an intellectual dimension; it requires courage as well as wisdom; it does not simply know, it also cares." *The Hesburgh Papers* (1979), p. 157.

L 12 "In a fast-changing society the real crisis is not one of authority but a crisis of vision that alone can inspire great leadership and create great morale in any society." *The Hesburgh Papers* (1979), p. 172.

L 13 "In times of great change, leadership is where you find it. This is especially true of moral and spiritual leadership." *The Hesburgh Papers* (179), p. 186.

L 14 "One can be forceful and humane at the same time, but I have to admit, having tried, it's not easy." Address, University of Portland, 1982.

L 15 "Spirit is the root of personality." *More Thoughts for Our Times* (1964), p. 7.

L 16 "When I have done something, it is over. I don't worry about what I said or how I said it. I do the best I can while I am doing it, and so be it." Quoted from *What Works for Me"* (1986), p. 153.

L 17 "It's my rule never, never to do anyone else's job. . . . When I select people for jobs, I want intelligent people. The worst combination a person can have is power and stupidity. . . ." Quoted from *What Works for Me* (1986), p. 162.

L 18 "My basic principle is that you don't make decisions because they are easy, you don't make them because they're cheap, you don't make them because they're popular; you make them because they are right." Quoted from *What Works for Me* (1986), p. 172.

L 19 "Success — real success — almost always has at least a minor ingredient of luck." Quoted from *What Works for Me* (1986), p. 173.

L 20 "The real leaders of this world all have a very deep sense of dedication — they're willing to give time to something. They don't say, I can't do it because I've got to play golf." Quoted from *What Works for Me* (1986), p. 174.

L 21 "I've often felt that you can really tell the quality of people by the things to which they give their precious time." Quoted from *What Works for Me* (1986), p. 175.

L 22 "The only way you can accomplish a lot is to concentrate on the one task you have at hand at the moment." Quoted from *What Works for Me* (1986), p. 176.

L 23 "Vision is the key to leadership. Unless you have a vision of where you're going, you are not going to get there." *USA Today*, January 18, 1981, p. 7.

L 24 "During my presidency at Notre Dame, I never appointed a football or basketball coach without a clear understanding — also involving the athletic director — that the coach's primordial responsibility is to insure that our rather strict rules will be enforced." Address at the Heisman Memorial Trophy Award, New York, N.Y., 1987.

CHAPTER 10

The Younger Generation

Father Hesburgh with a group of students on the Notre Dame campus, 1977

YG 1 "The world has had its fill of brilliant men who are immoral, and good men who are stupid." Address at the Universal Notre Dame Night, Washington, D.C., 1953.

YG 2 "Are we really doing all we might do to redeem and reorder and revivify the world in which we live today?" *Patterns for Educational Growth* (1958), p. 30.

YG 3 "Whatever you do in the days to come, you may be sure of this one basic fact of life: your life will be as significant as those things to which you dedicate your days." Commencement Address, University of Rhode Island, 1960.

YG 4 "Did you ever stop to think that a hundred years ago you were nothing, if not a thought in the infinite mind of God of someone who could be and would be some day. A hundred years hence you will, I believe, still be someone, somewhere, although for all that, only a statistic or a memory here on earth." Commencement Address, University of Rhode Island, 1960.

YG 5 "All of our lives are just about what we, with the grace of God, make them, and what we make of our lives reflects the goals or the values that we cherish and seek and establish throughout our days." Commencement Address, University of Rhode Island, 1960.

YG 6 "Take a quick look at the goals that emanate from Madison Avenue — they are pleasant to the touch, the taste, the eye — but by any ultimate standard they lack substance." Commencement Address, University of Rhode Island, 1960.

YG 7 "Passion for justice will or will not be a value in your life. If it is, it will ennoble you and others, if it is not, injustice will degrade others and you, too." Commencement Address, University of Rhode Island, 1960.

YG 8 "Something that is of dire need in the world today is a capacity for dedication, sacrifice, and hard work geared to excellence of performance." Commencement Address, University of Rhode Island, 1960.

YG 9 "Without high dedication and excellent performance in every age, there would have been no great religious or educational leaders, no outstanding scholars, artists, statesmen, scientists, doctors, lawyers, businessmen or engineers, no, not even any good husbands or wives, fathers or mothers." Commencement Address, University of Rhode Island, 1960.

YG 10 "There is nothing wrong, of course, in the material amenities of our day. But to make their acquisition and enjoyment the end all of human existence is a folly worth avoiding like the plague." Commencement Address, Massachusetts Institute of Technology, 1962.

YG 11 "We will not be judged by our degrees, but by our lives." Baccalaureate Address, St. Mary's College, 1962.

YG 12 "Wherever your path leads you, may it bring you to the true happiness that comes only to those who have learned that the measure of love is to love God and men without measure." Commencement Address, University of Wyoming, 1964.

YG 13 "Those who do not understand history are condemned to repeat the mistakes of the past." *More Thoughts for Our Times* (1964), p. 41.

YG 14 "Nothing has really happened to you if you are today a colorless, neutral, or uncommitted person." Commencement Address, Providence College, 1968.

YG 15 "I do not know where your paths will lead each of you in the days ahead. The place to which you go is nowhere near as important as what you do when you get there." Commencement Address, Providence College, 1968.

YG 16 "I would like to say of the younger generation what Frenchmen are purported to say of women: *vive la difference* — long live the difference between generations. We need it. They do, too." Commencement Address, Michigan State University, 1968.

YG 17 "Maybe the world of youth is too good to be true and lasting. Maybe instead of being so concerned about the idealism, the generosity, and the vehemence of youth, we should rather mourn the fact that youth passes all too quickly into the grim life of adulthood, when we find it so difficult to really love what is good and hate what is evil." Commencement Address, Michigan State University, 1968.

YG 18 "The world needs energy, imagination, concern, idealism, dedication, commitment, service. The world, with all its problems, gets all too little of these great human qualities from the older generation." Commencement Address, Michigan State University, 1968.

YG 19 "One bit of advice our most active students need to hear from faculty today is that action is most fruitful when it is backed up, not by emotion, or mass hysteria, or noise, or violence, but by intelligent and competent leadership which is the fruit of a good education that is taken seriously during the years when it is available." Commencement Address, Michigan State University, 1968.

YG 20 "Saints, like stars, are points of reference. They guide us on our way, although few reach them." Notre Dame Law School Address, University of Notre Dame, 1969.

YG 21 "Let your educated mind and heart be a light in the darkness of the world. Be bridge builders over the chasms that separate people, the young and old, the rich and poor, the black and white, the ignorant and the learned. Go out from here as one who both knows and loves, one who has cherished wisdom and built character, and, above all, one who has learned to give of self." Address at the Aquinas Assembly, Kings College, 1972.

YG 22 "Our younger generation will not wait forever for peaceful solutions to this burning problem of human equality. The young have only one life to live here on earth and it is now before them, filled with a whole series of tantalizing opportunities. They know that the human situation need not be what it is, as we permit it to be. . . . The younger generation is being constantly and strongly tempted to violence, violence that solves nothing and deepens human misery, even the misery of the young." *The Humane Imperative* (1974), p. 28.

YG 23 "One of the greatest intellectual and moral needs of mankind is to find a workable rationale for continuity in times of change." Ditchley Foundation Lecture, Oxfordshire, England, 1974.

YG 24 "Human ingenuity in the face of crisis has been one of mankind's greatest glories." Ditchley Foundation Lecture, Oxfordshire, England, 1974.

YG 25 "Puny dreams, low aspirations, half-hearted efforts are unworthy of us, both as a people and as a nation." Commencement Address, University of Denver, 1976.

YG 26 "Age alone is no real guarantee of quality unless one is considering red wine or cheese." *The Hesburgh Papers* (1979), p. 37.

YG 27 "Change has often been described as a condition of life — what does not change, dies." *The Hesburgh Papers* (1979), p. 69.

YG 28 ". . . we must take some chances and have more faith in this younger generation and have more understanding of their concerns." *The Hesburgh Papers* (1979), p. 78.

YG 29 "If we read the signs of the times, young people to-day have a very special approach to the ultimate religious reality, which is union with God. We, in our day, realized this by the sacramental approach. They have discovered a new sacrament — service to the poor and the disadvantaged. Why disparage their desires to find in service to others a new form of prayer?" *The Hesburgh Papers* (1979), p. 79.

YG 30 "Whatever you value, be committed to it and let nothing distract you from this goal. . . . Compassion means that you suffer with all who suffer, the hungry, the ignorant, the poor, the homeless, the hopeless, the sick, all those who suffer injustice, all who need understanding and help." *The Hesburgh Papers* (1979), p. 124.

YG 31 "Consecration means that we take gifts we have from God and give them back in service. . . . Commitment, compassion, and consecration. Three words, these are the sum of my free advice. May you find them sturdy companions." *The Hesburgh Papers* (1979), p. 125.

YG 32 "It is always better to revitalize a basically good system than to destroy it violently while having nothing with which to replace it. And, if that is true of our universities, it is even more true of our families, of our cities, of our nation and our world. . . . The young can make and should contribute to man's perennial task of remaking the world, especially since they are half of the world that needs remaking. . . . It is likely that history will repeat itself and the gap between the generations will never be completely bridged by understanding, but I like to believe that there are other workable bridges, at least more workable than anything in common use today, and their names are laughter and love." *The Hesburgh Papers* (1979), p. 137-38.

YG 33 "Indeed, I can think of no better way of redeeming this tragic world today than by love and laughter. Too many of the young have forgotten how to laugh, and too many of the elders have forgotten how to love. Would not the dark tragedy of our life be lightened if only we could all learn to laugh more easily at ourselves and to love one another?" *The Hesburgh Papers* (1979), p. 138.

YG 34 "A large part of the difficulty of understanding the younger generation today is the very real difficulty of understanding ourselves and the world-in-change in which we all live." *The Hesburgh Papers* (1979), p. 142.

YG 35 "Communication between the generations is reversed; parents can and must learn from their children, who are more at home in the present world than the parents are." *The Hesburgh Papers* (1979), p. 143.

YG 36 "Possibly they (the younger generation) are our salvation in these troubling times, when we of the older generation may have too much of the baggage of the past to make the clear-cut decisions that are too easy for the young, who bring to our present situation a freshness of the dawn and unencumbered judgement, a new insight. . . . They are at times very perceptive and at times very stupid; they have insight and blindness; their idealism is faulted by their inherent lack of discipline, and they are, like all young people of all times, more given to the activism of the moment than to the contemplation and wisdom that make action meaningful." *The Hesburgh Papers* (1979), p. 144.

YG 37 "The older generation today infuriates the younger by projecting this as a world of law and order." *The Hesburgh Papers* (1979), p. 145.

YG 38 "Youth especially has much to offer — idealism, generosity, dedication, and service." *The Hesburgh Papers* (1979), p. 165.

YG 39 "There is no genuine learning, for example, without the humble submission of intelligence to the demands and discipline of plodding inquiry, in community with others who do not allow one to do simply as one pleases." *The Hesburgh Papers* (1979), p. 179.

YG 40 "The mind, like muscles, must be exercised to grow." Commencement Address, University of Seattle, 1981.

YG 41 "Students have a highly developed radar that quickly separates out the sincere from the phony and the conviction from the posturing." Banquet Address, Loretto Heights College, 1982.

YG 42 "Don't be afraid to commit yourself to love, commit yourself to giving, commit yourself to dedication, commit yourself to devotion." Baccalaureate Address, Colgate University, 1983.

YG 43 "Don't be like some Americans who simply live in their own little world, enjoy their superabundance and never think about the rest of the people and what they're up against. Be the kind of person who not only understands the injustices of this life, but is also willing to do something about them." Commencement Address, University of Nebraska-Lincoln, 1986.

Values, HE 21, HE 33, HE 38, PS 21;
    and science, ST 29; eternal, HND 13, MV 3, PS 18;
    in liberal education, HE 20; learning of, HE 36;
    moral, HND 20, MV 6, MV 9; sense of, MV 5,
    MV 15, MV 16, MV 17; spiritual, PS 17, PS 25;
    teaching of, MV 18
Virtue, MV 14, HND 20
Vision, HE 14, L 12; and leadership, L 23;
    and faith, PS 39, PS 40
Voluntarism, S 11, S 12, S 13
Volunteer associations, S 10
Wisdom, HE 3, HE 40, HND 1, HND 2, HND 8,
    HND 21, MV 14, PS 5; work of, PS 2
Women, HR 18
Work, L 22; eternal value of, PS 8
Younger generation, YG 16, YG 28
Youth, MV 8, YG 17